TREASURE TIME FINALE
Leader Manual

Treasure Hunt Bible Adventure

Group
Loveland, Colorado

Treasure Time Finale Leader Manual

Copyright © 1999 Group Publishing, Inc.

All rights reserved. No part of this book may be reproduced in any manner whatsoever without prior written permission from the publisher, except where noted on handouts and in the case of brief quotations embodied in critical articles and reviews. For information, write Permissions, Group Publishing, Inc., Dept. PD, P.O. Box 481, Loveland, CO 80539.

Credits
Treasure Hunt Bible Adventure Coordinator: Jody Brolsma
Authors: Cindy S. Hansen and Julie Meiklejohn
Chief Creative Officer: Joani Schultz
Copy Editor: Janis Sampson
Art Director: Kari K. Monson
Cover Art Director: Lisa Chandler
Cover Designers: Becky Hawley and Jerry Krutar
Computer Graphic Artist: Nighthawk Design
Cover Photographer: Craig DeMartino
Illustrator: Amy Bryant
Rain Forest Art: Pat Allen
Rain Forest Art Photographer: Linda Bohm
Choreographer: Cindy S. Hansen
Audio Engineer: Steve Saavedra
Video Engineer: Mark Toutge
Production Manager: Peggy Naylor

Unless otherwise noted, Scripture taken from the HOLY BIBLE, NEW INTERNATIONAL VERSION®. Copyright © 1973, 1978, 1984 by International Bible Society. Used by permission of Zondervan Publishing House. All rights reserved.

ISBN 0-7644-9913-0
Printed in the United States of America.
10 9 8 7 6 5 4 3 2 1   00 99

CONTENTS

Welcome to Treasure Hunt Bible Adventure! 5

Your Contribution to
   Treasure Hunt Bible Adventure..............................6

The Overview 8

Gearing Up for the Adventure! 10

Treasure Chest Quest: Clue Crew Capers
   That Keep Everyone Guessing! 13

DAY 1 (The Bible shows us the way to trust.) 18

DAY 2 (The Bible shows us the way to love.) 23

DAY 3 (The Bible shows us the way to pray.) 27

DAY 4 (The Bible shows us the way to Jesus.) 32

DAY 5 (The Bible shows us the way to live.) 36

Welcome to TREASURE HUNT BIBLE ADVENTURE!

X marks the spot…for VBS excitement! Grab your compass, dust off your binoculars, and be sure your flashlight has batteries. You're hot on the trail to Treasure Hunt Bible Adventure, where kids discover Jesus—the biggest treasure of all! Your young adventurers will explore how the Bible maps the way to amazing riches, showing us the way to trust, love, pray, and live. Kids begin each day's treasure hunt by doing fun motions to new as well as familiar Bible songs during Treasure Hunt Sing & Play. Then they'll join with their Clue Crews to create cool treasures at Craft Cave, view *Chadder's Treasure Hunt Adventure* video, experience "vine" dining at Treasure Treats, dig into Bible Exploration, and monkey around at Jungle Gym Games. Then everyone will come together to participate in Treasure Time Finale.

Treasure Time Finale is just one of seven Discovery Sites kids will visit each day of their Treasure Hunt Bible Adventure. At each Discovery Site, kids will experience the daily Bible Point in a new way. During Treasure Time Finale, kids will sing upbeat songs that correspond to the daily Bible Point, and they'll actively participate in a daily presentation that reinforces the lesson.

Leading Treasure Time Finale is easy and fun!

You'll enjoy your role and be most successful as a Treasure Time Finale Leader if you

- enjoy being in front of people,
- are a bit of a ham,
- are an expressive storyteller,
- like to laugh and have a good sense of humor,
- encourage and affirm kids' participation in each day's Treasure Time Finale, and
- model God's love in everything you say and do.

Your Contribution

It may be helpful to meet with the Treasure Hunt Director and go over the supply list. Let the director know what supplies you have or can collect on your own and what supplies you'll need to purchase or collect from church members. Open communication makes your job even easier!

Field Test Findings

You'll notice that Treasure Hunt Bible Adventure doesn't include a program for kids to perform for their parents. At our field test, leaders found it refreshing and relaxing to not have the busyness and pressure of a "performance." And the kids enjoyed singing just to praise God and have fun! If you want parents to get a peek at Treasure Hunt Bible Adventure, invite them to each day's closing program.

Your Contribution to TREASURE HUNT BIBLE ADVENTURE

Here's what's expected of you before, during, and after Group's Treasure Hunt Bible Adventure:

Before TREASURE HUNT BIBLE ADVENTURE

☘ Attend scheduled Discovery Site Leader training.

☘ Pray for the kids who will attend your church's Treasure Hunt Bible Adventure.

☘ Ask your Treasure Hunt Director (otherwise known as your church's VBS director!) what you should wear each day. Discovery Site Leader T-shirts (available from Group Publishing or your local Christian bookstore) help kids identify you—and help you identify other Discovery Site Leaders. If your Treasure Hunt Director doesn't order T-shirts, you may want to agree on another easily recognizable uniform, such as a colorful T-shirt, khaki shorts, and a tan explorer's vest.

☘ Read through this Treasure Time Finale manual.

☘ Consult with other Discovery Site Leaders to recruit helpers for each day's show. You'll need at least one other person each day to help you manage props, sound, and lighting. A few jobs should be rehearsed ahead of time, but most can be completed by anyone who's available. Since preschool children need close adult supervision, don't plan on enlisting the Preschool Bible Treasure Land Leader unless absolutely necessary.

You may want to enlist the Treasure Hunt Sing & Play Leader as your permanent assistant, since he or she will already be leading songs during each show. The Treasure Hunt Sing & Play Leader can help you with cuing the audiocassette or CD, staging kids who volunteer to participate in each show, and turning the lights on and off. Other Discovery Site Leaders can fill in as needed.

☘ Set up and check all equipment to make sure it's working properly.

☘ Practice each day's program three times:
once at home by yourself,
once at home in front of an honest audience (or a mirror), and
once in your designated Discovery Site location with all the equipment up and running.

During TREASURE HUNT BIBLE ADVENTURE

♣ Build enthusiasm for Treasure Time Finale by interacting with kids throughout the day. Visit other Discovery Sites to get a feel for what kids are doing.

♣ Help the Treasure Hunt Sing & Play Leader demonstrate the motions to "I've Found Me a Treasure" on Day 1.

♣ To help create a fun atmosphere and reinforce Bible learning, play the *Treasure Hunt Sing & Play* audiocassette or CD as kids enter and leave the room.

♣ Cue the *Skits & Drama* audiocassette for the days you need it. The Bible Exploration Leader will also use this audiocassette, so be sure to make plans to deliver and retrieve it at the appropriate times.

♣ Cue the *Treasure Hunt Sing & Play* audiocassette or CD to the first song you'll be singing during each day's Treasure Time.

♣ Start each day's Treasure Time Finale on time.

♣ When using the *Treasure Hunt Sing & Play* audiocassette or CD, be a pro! Fade the music in and out slowly, rather than turning it on and off abruptly.

♣ Have fun as you lead kids through each day's Treasure Time Finale activities. Be sure to smile a lot!

♣ Be flexible. You may need to adapt the Treasure Time Finale material to fit your facility or to accommodate a longer or shorter time frame.

♣ Allow a few minutes for announcements at the beginning of each day's Treasure Time Finale.

♣ Repeat the daily Bible Point often. It's important to say the Bible Point just as it's written. Kids will be listening for each day's Bible Point so they can respond by shouting "Eureka!" Each day's Treasure Time Finale program suggests ways to include the Bible Point.

♣ Invite parents and grandparents to come *every day* and join in the Treasure Time Finale festivities. You may also be asked to help your Treasure Hunt Director plan an additional closing program using various Treasure Time Finale activities.

After TREASURE HUNT BIBLE ADVENTURE

♣ Return equipment to its proper place. Return the *Skits & Drama* audiocassette to your Treasure Hunt Director.

♣ Throughout the year you can help kids discover even more about Jesus by
- phoning neighborhood kids who participated in your Treasure Hunt Bible Adventure program,
- sending Treasure Hunt Bible Adventure follow-up postcards, and
- repeating segments of your Treasure Time Finale in your Sunday school or midweek programs.

Your Contribution: A CLUE FOR YOU!

As the Treasure Time Finale Leader, you can also double as photographer (or videographer). Early in the week, follow the kids with a camera loaded with slide film (or a video camera). Capture kids playing games, making or displaying their crafts, and enjoying Treasure Treats. Have your film developed, then choose slides for an optional five-minute slide presentation during Day 5's Treasure Time Finale. Kids and parents will love seeing themselves on "the big screen."

You may also want to take posed photographs of individuals and Clue Crews. Treasure Treats is a great time to line up kids for these photos. (Treasure Hunt Bible Adventure photo frames are available from Group Publishing or your local Christian bookstore.) At the end of the week, you can sell your framed photos to raise money to offset the costs of this year's program. Or you can give them away to participating families as an outreach and follow-up tool.

TREASURE HUNT BIBLE ADVENTURE OVERVIEW

This is what everyone else is doing! At Treasure Hunt Bible Adventure, the daily Bible Point is carefully integrated into each Discovery Site activity to reinforce Bible learning. Treasure Time Finale is an important part of kids' overall learning experience.

	BIBLE POINT	BIBLE STORY	BIBLE VERSE	TREASURE HUNT SING & PLAY	CRAFT CAVE	JUNGLE GYM GAMES
DAY 1	The Bible shows us the way to trust.	Peter walks to Jesus on the Sea of Galilee (Matthew 14:22-33).	"Do not let your hearts be troubled. Trust in God" (John 14:1a).	• He's Got the Whole World in His Hands • The B-I-B-L-E • Where Do I Go? • I've Found Me a Treasure (chorus and verse 1)	**Craft** Jungle Gel **Application** Kids need to trust the Craft Cave Leader that Jungle Gel really works. In the same way, we need to trust God when things in life seem impossible.	**Games** • Swamp Squish • Peter's Windy Walk • The River Bend • Treasure Tag • Pass-Along Peter **Application** The Bible teaches us that God is powerful and that we can trust him.
DAY 2	The Bible shows us the way to love.	Jesus washes the disciples' feet (John 13:1-17).	"A new command I give you: Love one another" (John 13:34a).	• Put a Little Love in Your Heart • I've Found Me a Treasure (add verse 2) • Jesus Loves Me	**Craft** Operation Kid-to-Kid Magnetic Bible Bookmarks **Application** Just as the magnet links the two children on the bookmark together, the Bible connects us with others around the world.	**Games** • Monkeys Love Bananas • Footrace • Gold Coin Keep-Away • Firefly Fling • Mosquito Net **Application** As the Bible shows us how to love, we can love others.
DAY 3	The Bible shows us the way to pray.	Jesus prays for his disciples and all believers, and then he is arrested (John 17:1–18:11).	"I pray also for those who will believe in me through their message, that all of them may be one" (John 17:20a-21b).	• Let Us Pray • Hey Now • I've Found Me a Treasure (add verse 3)	**Craft** Surprise Treasure Chests **Application** When kids open the treasure chest, they'll be surprised at the "riches" inside. When we open our hearts to God in prayer, we'll be surprised by his loving response.	**Games** • Savor the Flavor • Centipede Scurry • Message Mime • It's a Jungle! • Flowers of Blessing **Application** It's easy to talk to God.
DAY 4	The Bible shows us the way to Jesus.	Jesus is crucified, rises again, and appears to Mary Magdalene (John 19:1–20:18).	"For God so loved the world that he gave his one and only Son, that whoever believes in him shall not perish but have eternal life" (John 3:16).	• He's Alive • Make Your Home in My Heart • Good News • Oh, How I Love Jesus • I've Found Me a Treasure (add verse 4)	**Craft** Good News Treasure Pouches **Application** The colorful beads on the Treasure Pouch will remind kids of the good news that Jesus died for our sins and rose again!	**Games** • Roll Away the Stone • Butterfly Breakout • Manic Monarchs • Jungle-Bird Jiggle • He Has Risen! **Application** Our lives can be changed because Jesus rose from the dead.
DAY 5	The Bible shows us the way to live.	Paul stands firm in his faith, even in a shipwreck (Acts 27:1-44).	"If you love me, you will obey what I command" (John 14:15).	• The B-I-B-L-E • Got a Reason for Livin' Again • I've Found Me a Treasure (entire song)	**Craft** Rain Forest Creatures **Application** Kids add color and "life" to Rain Forest Creatures just as God's Word adds color and meaning to our lives.	**Games** • Man-Overboard Tag • Out to Sea • Snake Swap • Crash Course • Cargo Toss **Application** Even when life seems scary or difficult, we can have confidence that God is in control.

This chart maps out the entire program at a glance. Refer to the chart to see how your Discovery Site activities supplement other activities and help kids discover Jesus—the greatest treasure of all.

TREASURE TREATS	CHADDER'S TREASURE HUNT THEATER	BIBLE EXPLORATION	TREASURE TIME FINALE
Snack Peter's Adventure Cakes **Application** Peter's adventure began when he trusted Jesus. Jesus wants us to trust him, too.	**Video Segment** Chadder and his friends begin searching for a hidden treasure. They stumble onto the deck of the SS Hope, where Wally the parrot warns them to watch out for Riverboat Bob. Chadder's afraid, so Ryan, the first mate, tells him to trust God. The kids go to Whistle Cave, followed by Ned and Pete, two scraggly sailors who want the treasure for themselves. The kids find the treasure map, moments before they're trapped by a cave-in! **Application** • Where do you turn when you're afraid? • How does the Bible help you trust in God? • Mark your Student Book at a Trust Verse.	**Peter Walks on Water** • Experience being in a ship during a storm. • Try walking on "water." • Discuss how Peter learned to trust Jesus.	• Watch how a pin can go into a balloon, without popping the balloon! • Use balloons to review the story of Peter walking on the water. • Receive gem treasures as reminders that we are precious to God.
Snack Love Chests **Application** Jesus showed love for his disciples when he washed their feet. Today's snack shows that love is a great treasure.	**Video Segment** Chadder sits in an old mine car, and the car takes off, racing through the cave. Near the cave exit stands Riverboat Bob. He hits the hand brake and Chadder goes flying, right into the boxes Ryan has been stacking on deck. Chadder thinks Ryan will be mad, but Ryan says he follows Jesus' example of showing love. Chadder leaves to look for his friends, but runs into Riverboat Bob instead! **Application** • Role play how you think Ryan will react to the mess Chadder made. • How can the Bible help you when it's hard to love someone? • How can the Love Verse you highlighted help you love this week?	**Jesus Washes the Disciples' Feet** • Go on a barefoot hunt to find the Upper Room. • Have their feet washed by their Clue Crew Leader. • Help wash their Clue Crew Leader's feet. • Help one another put their shoes back on.	• See how someone shows unexpected love to the Treasure Time Finale Leader. • Receive heart locks and keys as treasures to remind them that loving actions open people's hearts.
Snack Prayer Treasure Mix **Application** Jesus' prayer teaches us to pray. The items in the Prayer Treasure Mix remind kids to pray about specific things.	**Video Segment** Chadder awakes in the mine and finds Hayley and Tim. They find a clue and decide to ask Ryan for help. The kids find Ryan in prayer, and Ryan shows them the Bible story of Jesus praying. Chadder wanders off, and Colonel Mike sees him and mistakes him for a scoundrel. Colonel Mike tells Chadder to walk the plank. **Application** • Pray in your crew for the child who'll receive your Spanish Bible. • Is there ever a time when you shouldn't pray? Explain. • How can you pray as Jesus taught?	**Jesus Prays** • Learn ways to pray for themselves. • Practice praying for various groups of people. • Create a mural with their hand prints to represent Jesus' prayer for all believers.	• Watch a skit about what it might be like for God to listen to our prayers. • Receive magnifying glass treasures as reminders that prayer brings us closer to God.
Snack Empty Tombs **Application** On the third day, Jesus' tomb stood empty. These scrumptious snacks are empty, too.	**Video Segment** Ryan explains that Chadder's a friend, and Colonel Mike points the kids toward the monkey tree. Chadder loses the map, but Ryan assures him that Jesus is the real treasure. The wind blows the map back again, and the hunt continues. The kids find the treasure chest, and Chadder finds the key to the chest hidden in the old tree. Just as they open the chest, Ned and Pete step up to steal the treasure. **Application** • How do you get to heaven? • How can knowing the treasure of Jesus change your life? • Why is it important to know about the treasure of Jesus?	**Mary Magdalene at the Empty Tomb** • Experience the sadness of the crucifixion. • Hear Mary tell how she searched for her lost treasure—Jesus—at the empty tomb. • Hear "Jesus" call their names; then draw crosses on their mural hand prints to thank God for Jesus.	• Pray; then give their sins to "Jesus" and watch as he makes the sins disappear. • Receive personal messages from their Clue Crew Leaders that Jesus loves them. • Receive three gold coin treasures as reminders that Jesus is the most valuable treasure we have.
Snack Sailboat Sandwiches **Application** When Paul faced a shipwreck, his trust in God helped him. We can live an adventurous life when we believe in God.	**Video Segment** Ned and Pete plan to take the treasure, but Riverboat Bob steps in to help. Bob reveals that he's been watching over the kids all along. Colonel Mike wants to throw Ned and Pete to the alligators, but Ryan convinces him to show God's love. Hayley, Tim, and Chadder fantasize about what they'll do with the treasure, but decide to give the money to Colonel Mike to help him bring supplies and Bibles to people along the river. **Application** • How can the Bible help you make decisions this week? • What do you think about giving your Spanish Bible away? Why? • When are times you can use the Bible verses you marked this week?	**Paul Is Shipwrecked** • Be "handcuffed," and led inside a prisoner's ship. • Hear a fellow prisoner tell about Paul's experience in the ship. • Experience a shipwreck. • Discuss how Paul's life was in God's control.	• Use a "chirping parrot" to experience the importance of working together to tell others about Jesus. • Present their Spanish translations of the Gospel of John as a special offering. • Receive a compass as a reminder that the Bible gives us direction in life.

Gearing Up for the Adventure!

GEARING UP FOR THE ADVENTURE!

A Clue for You!

If at all possible, meet in a room with good acoustics. Avoid meeting in a gymnasium or other tiled room, which tends to be "echo-y" and noisy.

Field Test Findings

At our field test, we had two enthusiastic teenagers who helped out as sound technicians. The children loved looking up to the soundboard to watch the "big kids" moving to the music and participating in the program. Not only were these high schoolers a great help to our Treasure Time Finale Leader, they were super examples of servanthood and God's love.

Discovery Site Preparation

♣ Work with the Treasure Hunt Director to select a room for Treasure Time Finale. You'll need a large room (such as a sanctuary or fellowship hall) that will accommodate your entire group. You may want to use the same room for both Treasure Time Finale and Treasure Hunt Sing & Play.

♣ Remove any items that might distract children. If you're meeting in your church's sanctuary, these might include attendance cards, hymnals, or pencils. Be sure to return all items to their proper places before your church's worship time!

♣ Clear the presentation area of unnecessary furniture.

♣ Set up (or have your church's sound technician set up) a microphone for yourself. Practice with the microphone so you'll know how to turn it on and remove it from its stand.

♣ Set up an audiocassette or CD player where you'll be able to reach it easily. Or ask another Discovery Site Leader to assist you in turning the music on and off. If you'd like to play the audiocassette or CD on your church's sound system, arrange for someone to be a "sound person" for you. Be sure to agree on a signal so you'll both know when it's time to start and stop the audiocassette or CD. If you can't use a sound system, plan to hold a microphone to the audiocassette or CD player's speaker so the music will be loud enough for everyone to hear.

♣ Decorate the Treasure Time Finale area to create a rain forest atmosphere. Use a variety of real and artificial plants, including artificial peace lilies, birds of

paradise, and hanging moss; carpet-roll tree trunks with crepe paper palm fronds; and vines made of rope and construction paper. Add stuffed-toy exotic animals and a Mylar-streamer waterfall. If you'll be using the same area for Treasure Hunt Sing & Play and the Treasure Time Finale, work together with the Treasure Hunt Sing & Play Leader to prepare the room. Use your creativity!

♣ Photocopy the Treasure Time Finale sign and arrow on the inside covers of this leader manual. Post the sign and arrow where they'll most effectively guide kids to the Treasure Time Finale area.

Discovery Site Supplies

Each day, you'll need
○ a Bible,
○ a microphone (if there are more than forty kids or if you're using a large room),
○ an audiocassette or CD player,
○ the *Treasure Hunt Sing & Play* audiocassette or CD (from the Treasure Hunt Sing & Play Leader),
○ a clock or a watch, and
○ a bamboo whistle* or another attention-getting device.

For Day 1, you'll need
○ nine-inch green and blue balloons* (one balloon per child),
○ large plastic trash bags,
○ a straight pin,
○ the *Skits & Drama* audiocassette* and a cassette player,
○ large plastic jewels* (one per child), and
○ two treasure chests.

For Day 2, you'll need
○ a large, clear plastic dropcloth (to cover a carpeted floor);
○ a large, unbreakable bowl filled with water;
○ several towels;
○ heart locks with keys* (one per child); and
○ two treasure chests.

A Clue For You!

When kids arrive for Treasure Time Finale, they'll probably start talking to their friends in their Clue Crews. If there are more than forty kids, you may need more than a bamboo whistle to get their attention. Using a microphone will prevent you from having to shout above kids' voices and will help your voice last all week.

A Clue For You!

Attention-getting signals let kids know it's time to stop what they're doing and look at you. You can use the bamboo whistle (available from Group Publishing or your local Christian bookstore) or another noisemaker of your choice. The bamboo whistle is easy to hear and provides a fun, exotic sound for your rain forest. Once kids are familiar with the signal, regaining their attention will become automatic. (By the time children arrive at your site, they should have already learned what the whistle means!)

Gearing Up for the Adventure!

Field Test Findings

We recommend two treasure chests for your Treasure Chest Quest—one for elementary and another for preschoolers. In our field test, we discovered that preschoolers were less likely to get crushed, pushed, or stepped on if they had their own treasure chest.

For Day 3, you'll need

- ○ simple costumes for the "Hailing the Chief" skit. Some costume possibilities include a wig and a scarf for the woman, a sport coat for the man, headphones for the young man, a bathrobe for the sleepy woman, and a baseball cap and teddy bear for the child.
- ○ a table and two chairs,
- ○ the *Skits & Drama* audiocassette* and a cassette player,
- ○ a simple magnifying glass* (one per child), and
- ○ two treasure chests.

For Day 4, you'll need

- ○ brightly colored slips of paper cut into various shapes (one per child);
- ○ two large paper bags;
- ○ a simple costume for the character of Jesus, such as a white sheet and a gold cloth strip to tie around the waist;
- ○ the *Skits & Drama* audiocassette* and a cassette player;
- ○ "gold" coins* (three per child); and
- ○ two treasure chests.

For Day 5, you'll need

- ○ slides, a slide projector, and a screen (if you decide to do a slide show);
- ○ poster board;
- ○ markers;
- ○ fifteen balloons;*
- ○ string;
- ○ a chirping parrot;*
- ○ the *Skits & Drama* audiocassette* and a cassette player;
- ○ compasses* (one per child);
- ○ two treasure chests;
- ○ Operation Kid-to-Kid posters from the Craft Cave Leader; and
- ○ a treasure chest to hold the Spanish translations of the Gospel of John.

*available from Group Publishing or your local Christian bookstore

Field Test Findings

For "Hailing the Chief" on Day 3, we didn't have a teddy bear handy, so our actor grabbed the Chadder Chipmunk puppet. Kids loved seeing Chadder Chipmunk in a new place, and the furry puppet added a great, lovable touch to the skit.

Discovery Site Safety Tips

♣ Tape down any microphone cords so children (and you!) won't trip over them.

♣ To avoid accidents or lost crafts, have kids keep their Craft Cave crafts on the floor or in their crew treasure bags when they're not using them.

♣ If possible, set all the action on a raised platform or stage. This will discourage children from standing on (and possibly falling off!) pews or chairs as they strain to see.

TREASURE CHEST QUEST:
Clue Crew Capers That Keep Everyone Guessing!

A treasure awaits you,
But what could it be?
Follow your clues
And soon you will see!

Treasure Chest Quest

Field Test Findings

This turned out to be a huge hit at our field test! The excitement grew daily as kids looked forward to guessing the "mystery" treasure! Not only did they appreciate the simple trinkets, but the clues were a dynamite way for Clue Crews to get acquainted and focus on a goal. The Treasure Chest Quest was a "gold mine!"

Reinforce the treasure hunt theme by setting up a daily Treasure Chest Quest for Clue Crews to solve. The Treasure Chest Quest builds excitement and anticipation each day while promoting teamwork, communication, and cooperation among Clue Crew members. Besides, kids will love receiving a simple "treasure" each day! This is an easy addition that will have tremendous impact on kids.

1. Simply photocopy the daily clues on pages 15-17, and cut them apart. You'll need one set of clues for each elementary Clue Crew. (Make your job even easier by color-coding each day's clues. Photocopy the clues on colored paper, then write in a matching color the day those clues will be used.)

2. Place the clues for each day in separate envelopes. Mark the envelopes clearly so you can identify when the clues will be used ("Day 1, Clue 1," for example).

3. Each day choose three Discovery Sites where kids will receive their clues. You may want to keep these Discovery Sites the same or change them every day to keep Clue Crews guessing! Have Discovery Site Leaders distribute clues to the Clue Keepers at the end of the lesson before kids head out to their next sites. Clue Crews can discuss their clues between Discovery Sites, while enjoying Treasure Treats, or as they wait for other crews to arrive at Treasure Time Finale. (You can prepare your clues several weeks in advance, then simply distribute them to Discovery Site Leaders each day!)

4. Create a large treasure chest by covering a box and lid with brown paper. Decorate the paper to look like a treasure chest, adding aluminum foil trim for hinges and locks. If you add a piece of foam or wood to create a false bottom, the treasure chest will appear to be filled to the top with riches! (Check with church members to see if anyone has two boxes that look like treasure chests—one to

A CLUE FOR YOU!

To simplify the Treasure Chest Quest even more, place one clue on the daily schedule before you photocopy the schedule. Then each Clue Crew will already have one clue to get them sleuthing!

Treasure Chest Quest

Field Test Findings

We had a great time playing up the anticipation factor! After each clue was read, we had kids rub their chins and say "hmm." Then we asked kids to perform a "drumroll" by patting on their legs. Finally we all "trumpeted" a fanfare as the chest was opened to reveal the treasure. Kids ate it up!

A Clue For You! Although preschoolers won't take part in solving the clues, *do* allow them to dig into the treasure chest for a special prize. You'll treasure the enormous smiles on their faces!

hold treasures for the elementary-age children and one to hold treasures for the preschoolers.)

5. Each day fill the treasure chests with the item listed under "Today's Treasure." (These items are available from Group Publishing or your local Christian bookstore.) Place the boxes at the front of your Treasure Time Finale meeting area. (Keep the chests closed until kids exit.)

6. As you give closing announcements after Treasure Time Finale, see if any Clue Crews have solved the mystery. Call up a Clue Keeper from one crew, and have him or her read aloud the clues. Then ask for guesses as to what's inside the treasure chest. Use the Treasure Tie-In to explain how the treasure ties with the daily Point. Announce that today's treasure will be available as kids file out of Treasure Time Finale.

It's that easy!

TREASURE CHEST QUEST CLUES

Day 1: The Bible shows us the way to trust.

Today's Treasure: Large, plastic jewels in a variety of colors

Treasure Tie-In: If you saw a diamond straight from the mine, you might not believe that it was valuable. When diamonds come from the mines, they're covered with rocks and dirt! It takes a skilled jeweler to shape, cut, and polish a gem to make it priceless. In the same way, we need to trust God, even when things look like they might not turn out. In God's hands, our problems can turn into priceless opportunities!

Clue: PROVERBS 8:10-11

Clue: April, June, and November—
Each month has a treasure
To help you remember.

Clue: To find this treasure
You have to dig deep.
Venture into a mine—
You may find some to keep!

Day 2: The Bible shows us the way to love.

Today's Treasure: Small heart-shaped lock with keys

Treasure Tie-In: Jesus' loving actions helped the disciples understand how he wanted them to treat others. In the same way, our actions can show God's love to those around us. Just as this key opens the heart lock, our love can open people's hearts and minds to help them know God better.

Clue: I'm easily broken
So take care of me.
And always remember
That love is the key.

Clue: You may find gold coins
Or treasures so rare;
But without one of these,
You may have to share!

Clue: There once was a woodsman of tin
Who lacked something beating within.
He went on a mission
To find what was missin'...
The movie will tell you the end!

Day 3: The Bible shows us the way to pray.

Today's Treasure: Small, plastic magnifying glass

Treasure Tie-In: A magnifying glass is fun because it helps us see things we normally can't. Prayer works in a similar way. When we talk with God, we learn more about God. Just as a magnifying glass helps us see things close up, prayer brings us closer to God.

Any good detective
And you treasure hunters, too,
Carry this along
So as not to miss a clue!

TINY CLUES YOU WON'T LOSE IF ME, YOU'LL USE!

"The better to see you with, my dear!"
The Wolf

Day 4: The Bible shows us the way to Jesus.

Today's Treasure: Three large, plastic gold coins per person

Treasure Tie-In: These gold coins remind us that Jesus is the real treasure, no matter where we live or what we do. Jesus is the most valuable thing we can have in life. Since we have such a valuable treasure in Jesus, we can share it with others who don't know about him. Today you'll get three gold coins—one to keep and two to give away. As you give them away, remember to share the greatest treasure of all—Jesus!

PSALM 19:10

Clink, plink,
Clank, plank—
Drop them in your piggy bank!

Full moon
Gold balloon
Lemon pie
Sun in sky

Permission to photocopy this page from Group's Treasure Hunt Bible Adventure: Treasure Time Finale granted for local church use. Copyright © Group Publishing, Inc., P.O. Box 481, Loveland, CO 80539.

Day 5: The Bible shows us the way to live.

Today's Treasure: Plastic compass

Treasure Tie-In: Since many forests aren't mapped out, it's easy for hikers and campers to get lost. That's why it's important to take along a compass. If we use a compass, we'll always know which direction we're headed. God's Word is a lot like a compass, helping us know which way to go in life. The words in the Bible always point us in the right direction!

 **NORTH, SOUTH, EAST, WEST—
USE THIS, OR YOU'LL HAVE TO GUESS.**

Can't find your way
Out in the woods?
Maybe you need
Proper
Assistance from
Something that
Surely will help!

Going round in circles?
This will point the way!
If you do not have one,
In the jungle you may stay!

BIBLE POINT

✼ The Bible shows us the way to trust.

BIBLE BASIS

Matthew 14:22-33. Peter walks to Jesus on the Sea of Galilee.

When Jesus called, "Come, follow me," Peter didn't hesitate to abandon his fishing nets in obedience. As Jesus' disciple, Peter listened to Jesus' teachings, watched Jesus heal the sick, and witnessed Jesus' power over wind and waves. He believed that Jesus was the Son of God. Perhaps that's why, on the stormy Sea of Galilee, when Jesus said, "Come," Peter ventured from the safety of a boat and walked toward Jesus. The water may have been cold, the waves may have been high, and the wind may have stung his face, but Peter knew that the safest place to be was with Jesus. When Peter became afraid and began to sink, "Immediately, Jesus reached out his hand and caught him." In the arms of Jesus, Peter learned to trust. He later wrote, "Cast all your anxiety on him because he cares for you" (1 Peter 5:7).

The disciple Peter is the perfect picture of our humanity and weakness; he reminds us how desperately we need Jesus. Children feel that need just as keenly as adults. They're familiar with the fear that accompanies life's "storms"—when parents divorce, friends move away, pets die, and classmates tease. The children at your VBS need to know that, in the midst of those hard times, Jesus is calling them to "come." And when children step out in faith, Jesus will be there with open arms, ready to catch them. Today's activities will encourage children to cast all their worries upon a loving, compassionate, and mighty God.

Day 1

Spotlight on Supplies

For today's treasure hunt, you'll need
- an audiocassette or CD player,
- the *Treasure Hunt Sing & Play* audiocassette or CD,
- a bamboo whistle or another attention-getting device,
- nine-inch green and blue balloons (inflated),
- large plastic trash bags,
- a straight pin,
- the *Skits & Drama* audiocassette and a cassette player,
- large plastic jewels (one per child), and
- two treasure chests.

Spotlight on Setup

At least twenty minutes prior to the Treasure Time Finale, blow up the balloons. You'll probably want to recruit as many helpers as you can find to help you! After the balloons are blown up, put a mix of green and blue balloons in plastic trash bags, and set the trash bags near the stage area. Recruit several helpers to pass out the balloons during the show.

Cue the *Treasure Hunt Sing & Play* audiocassette or CD to "Where Do I Go?"

Recruit an assistant to help you with the experiment, and show him or her how to stick a pin into a balloon near the place the balloon is tied off. Using this technique, the balloon won't pop! (You'll want to practice this ahead of time!)

It's Treasure Time!

While you're waiting for crews to arrive from their Discovery Sites, say: **While we're waiting for everyone to get here, let's sing some songs! Let's start by singing the song "Where Do I Go?" That way, when people hear us singing, they'll know they "go" here for our finale!** Lead kids in welcoming the Treasure Hunt Sing & Play Leader and sing "Where Do I Go?" Join in as everyone sings and does the motions to this uplifting song. Ask:

- **Do we have everyone here? Do we have our whole group here?**

Say: **We need our whole group here before we start, so let's sing "He's Got the Whole World in His Hands" together.** After everyone has arrived, say: **Now that our whole group is here—welcome!**

When everyone is seated, say: **We're so glad you're here at Treasure Hunt Bible Adventure. I'm** [your name], **your Treasure Time Finale Leader, and I'm here to welcome you to our very first Treasure Time Finale.**

At Treasure Hunt Bible Adventure, we'll experience a wealth of fun-filled closing shows to help us learn more about Jesus—the

---

A CLUE FOR YOU!

It's a good idea to go over the motions for the songs again, as the preschool crews don't attend Treasure Hunt Sing & Play on the first day.

Day 1

greatest treasure of all! We'll also learn more about how the Bible maps our way to amazing riches! Be sure your crew gets here on time for this valuable event at Treasure Hunt Bible Adventure.

✡ BIBLE POINT

Today we learned that ✡ **the Bible shows us the way to trust.** (Eureka!) **Let's celebrate by singing about the person you've learned about this morning—Peter!**

Have the Treasure Hunt Sing & Play Leader lead kids in singing "I've Found Me a Treasure."

Ask:

● **In order for Peter to walk on the water, what did he have to do?** (Trust Jesus; step out onto the water; keep his eyes on Jesus.)

Say: **When Peter trusted Jesus and kept his eyes on Jesus, he could do something impossible—he walked on water!** Ask:

● **What happened when Peter took his eyes off Jesus?** (He sank; he started to fall in the water.)

Say: **When Peter got afraid and took his eyes off Jesus, he started to sink, didn't he? But Jesus helped him up, just like the way that Jesus always helps us up when we find it hard to trust.**

At first, Peter thought that walking on the water would be impossible, but he kept his eyes on Jesus, and he did it! Keep that thought in mind as we try an experiment. I need a volunteer to help me with this experiment.

Select an older child as a volunteer, and have him or her come up to join you. Ask for the volunteer's name, and say: [Child's name] **is going to help me show you this experiment. I'm going to give** [child's name] **a balloon and a pin.** Ask the group:

● **What do you think will happen if** [child's name] **sticks the pin into the balloon?** (It'll pop; it'll be loud!)

Say: **Let's try it on the count of three.** Lead the group in counting to three, and then have the volunteer stick the pin into the side of the balloon. The balloon will pop. Say: **Oh! It popped!** [Child's name], **thank you so much for helping. Let's try this one more time. Can I have another volunteer come up and try it?**

Select another volunteer, ask his or her name, and provide another balloon and pin. Say: **Now** [child's name] **will try to stick the pin into the balloon. Let's count to three.** Again lead the group in counting to three, and then have the volunteer stick the pin into the side of the balloon. Of course, it will pop. Say: **Oh! It popped again! Thank you,** [child's name], **for helping me out. Now I need** [adult helper's name] **to come up and try this just one more time.** Hand the helper a balloon and a pin, and ask the group:

● **What if I told you that if you just trust,** [helper's name] **can stick the pin into the balloon without popping it? Would you believe me?** Answers will vary.

Say: **Raise your hand if you think that's impossible!** Give kids a moment to raise their hands, and then say: **Raise your hand if you trust and think that** [helper's name] **can stick the pin into the balloon and not pop it.** Give kids a moment to raise their hands.

Then say: **Well, on the count of three,** [helper's name] **is going to try it!** Lead the group in counting to three, and then have the helper stick the pin into the balloon near the point where it's tied off. The balloon won't pop. Say: **Wow! It didn't pop!** Have the helper hold the balloon up so kids can see the pin sticking out of the top. Say: **Now I'm going to tell you what happened. The reason it was possible for** [helper's name] **to stick a pin into a balloon without the balloon popping was because he** [or she] **turned the balloon a different way and stuck the pin into the balloon right where the tie is. There's a lot of extra material there, so the balloon wouldn't pop.**

You know we've all had experiences with balloons. You knew that a pin would pop the first two balloons. When I told you to just trust that a pin wouldn't pop the third balloon, a lot of you said, "That's impossible!" But because [helper's name] **turned the balloon a different way, he** [or she] **could stick the pin into the balloon without popping it.**

That's just like Peter in our Bible story today. Everyone knew that a person couldn't walk on water—it was impossible and the person would sink. But when Peter turned his eyes another way—he turned his eyes toward Jesus and trusted him completely—he could do it!

Say: **In a moment you're each going to get a balloon, and we're going to use those balloons to do a prayerful reflection about trusting God. But first I'd like a few volunteers to come up and demonstrate what we're going to do.** Have four or five volunteers join you up front, and give each one a balloon. Make sure that some volunteers have green balloons and some have blue balloons.

Say: **When I say the word "afraid," people with blue balloons will wave them in the air up high.** Have volunteers with blue balloons wave them in the air. **When I say the word "trust," people with green balloons will wave them slowly in the air up high.** Have volunteers with green balloons wave them in the air. **When I say "Jesus," move all the balloons slowly and close to the ground. When I say "storm," wave all the balloons high and fast.** Let volunteers demonstrate.

Say: **OK. Now we're going to give each of you a balloon so we can do this together. When you get your balloon, hold it tightly, and be careful with it. You can take it home to show your parents and friends the experiment we did and tell them about trusting Jesus.** Have your helpers distribute balloons to kids. When everyone has a balloon, make sure kids are seated, and say: **Now let's be in a mood of prayer for this activity. That will help us review what we've learned today.** Play "Rain Forest Sounds" from the *Skits & Drama* audiocassette during the reflection.

Field Test Findings

In our field test, we distributed the balloons before demonstrating the actions. Needless to say, we had a mild "disturbance" of our own! Wait to distribute balloons until kids understand the motions and you're ready for them to move. You'll love the "wavy" effect of this activity!

Day 1

Say: **On that windy night in the boat, Peter and the other disciples were <u>afraid</u>.** Pause for blue balloons to wave. **They were so <u>afraid</u>.** Pause. **What were they supposed to do? They were supposed to <u>trust</u>.** Pause for green balloons to wave. **In that <u>storm</u>** (pause for all balloons to wave quickly) **Peter kept his eyes on <u>Jesus</u>.** Pause for all balloons to wave slowly. **Today, sometimes we're <u>afraid</u>.** Pause for blue balloons to wave. **What can we do? We're supposed to <u>trust</u>.** Pause for green balloons to wave. **We can <u>trust</u>** (pause for green balloons to wave) **in <u>Jesus</u>.** Pause for all balloons to wave slowly. **And no matter what tough times or <u>storms</u>** (pause) **we're facing, if we keep our eyes on <u>Jesus</u>** (pause), **<u>Jesus</u>** (pause) **will help us through.**

Now let's pray together. Hold your balloon in your lap, close your eyes, and bow your head. Pray: **Dear Jesus, we thank you that when we keep our eyes on you and trust you, you help us through the storms and tough times in life. Help us to remember to always keep our eyes on you and trust you no matter what good times or tough times we face. Thank you, Jesus. Amen.**

✸ BIBLE POINT

Say: **Now get your balloons ready because we're going to use them as we sing another song—"The B-I-B-L-E"! Remember, ✸ the Bible shows us the way to trust!** (Eureka!) **The Bible tells us about Peter, and it tells us about many other people who trusted Jesus.** Have the Treasure Hunt Sing & Play Leader lead kids in singing "The B-I-B-L-E" using the balloons to "punctuate" the arm motions.

After the song, say: **You can take your balloon home with you. When you get home, find a pin and stick it into the balloon near the tie. You'll amaze your friends and family members because the balloon won't pop! Then tell them how ✸ the Bible shows us the way to trust** (Eureka!) **just like Peter.**

✸ BIBLE POINT

TREASURE CHEST QUEST

Call a volunteer to the front to read aloud each clue. To build excitement, lead kids in saying "hmm" after each clue is read; then lead them in a "drumroll" and a "trumpet fanfare" as the chest is opened. Use the Treasure Tie-In on page 15 to help kids connect Today's Treasure to the Bible Point. Then invite the Treasure Hunt Director to make announcements, pray, and dismiss kids in an orderly manner to get their treasures from the treasure chest.

Have preschoolers remain seated until their parents or caregivers come and get them, and distribute their treasures from a second treasure chest.

Play "He's Got the Whole World in His Hands" from the *Treasure Hunt Sing & Play* audiocassette or CD as kids exit.

BIBLE POINT

✿ The Bible shows us the way to love.

BIBLE BASIS

John 13:1-17. Jesus washes the disciples' feet.

Jesus knew that his time on earth was coming to an end. His purpose would soon be accomplished, and he could return to heaven, to the side of the Father. Jesus' time with the disciples was coming to an end too. These followers, who gave up everything to follow Jesus and learn from him, must now carry his message to the world. What parting words would Jesus leave with them? How could he express his love for them and prepare them for the challenges ahead? Jesus' words were almost unnecessary, for his actions were unforgettable. The Son of God lowered himself to the position of a servant and washed his disciples' dusty feet. In this one simple act, Jesus demonstrated the depth of his love and modeled the servant's heart he desired in his followers.

It goes against human nature to put the needs of others ahead of our own. Our culture says to "look out for number one." We read magazines with titles such as Self and Moi. And we eat at restaurants where we can have it our way. Our world sends a self-centered and egocentric message to children, as well. That's why the children at your VBS can learn so much from Jesus' demonstration of love and humility. In today's activities, kids will experience the power of loving others through selfless acts. Children will discover that Jesus' actions are as unforgettable today as they were for the disciples nearly two thousand years ago.

Day 2

Spotlight on Supplies

For today's treasure hunt, you'll need
- an audiocassette or CD player,
- the *Treasure Hunt Sing & Play* audiocassette or CD,
- a large, clear plastic dropcloth (to cover a carpeted floor);
- a large, unbreakable bowl filled with water;
- several towels;
- heart locks with keys (one for each child); and
- two treasure chests.

Spotlight on Setup

Spread the plastic dropcloth on the floor of your stage area (if it's carpeted). Fill the large bowl with water, and set it on a small table or stand in the middle of the stage. Set the towels on the floor nearby.

Recruit the Treasure Hunt Director, the church pastor, or another "authority figure" to help you present the scenario on page 25.

It's Treasure Time!

While you're waiting for crews to arrive from their Discovery Sites, say: **While we're waiting for everyone to get here, let's sing some songs! Let's start by singing the song "Where Do I Go?" That way, when people hear us singing, they'll know where to go for our finale!** Lead kids in welcoming the Treasure Hunt Sing & Play Leader and sing "Where Do I Go?" Join in as everyone sings and does the motions to this uplifting song. Ask:

- **Do we have everyone here? Do we have our whole group here?**

Say: **We need our whole group here before we start, so let's sing "He's Got the Whole World in His Hands." together.** After everyone has arrived, say: **Now that our whole group is here—welcome!**

After everyone is seated, ask another leader to rewind the audiocassette or cue the CD to "Jesus Loves Me" as you're welcoming all the crew members.

Blow your bamboo whistle and say: **Welcome to Day 2 of Treasure Time Finale. What did you like the best today at Treasure Hunt Bible Adventure?** Allow kids to respond.

✣ **BIBLE POINT**

Today we learned that ✣ the Bible shows us the way to love. (Eureka!) **Let's sing a song that tells us more about our Point. Because Jesus loves us so much, we love others. Let's sing "Jesus Loves Me."**

Join in as everyone sings. After the song, say: **Today you learned a story from our treasure map, the Bible.** Ask:

- **What can you tell me about the story you learned?** (Jesus washed his friends' feet; Jesus showed love.)

Then say: **In today's story Jesus—the Son of God—took a bowl of water** (lift the bowl of water up) **and washed his disciples' feet. The job was a servant's job. Just like a maid would clean a house, a servant in Jesus' time would wash people's feet.** Hold up the bowl of water again as if you're going to continue speaking. Suddenly "trip" and drop the bowl, spilling the water all over the floor. Say: **Oh no! Look what happened! I can't believe I did that! I'm so embarrassed! Look at this mess!** From the back of the room, have the "authority figure" ask: "Is everything OK up there?"

Say (in a frantic voice): **Oh…it's fine! Everything's fine! We're just…uh…having a little finale here!** Say to the group in a stage whisper: **Oh no! What am I going to do?** Motion to kids in the front, and say: **Can you kids come and stand in front of this mess? Maybe you can block me while I clean it up. Oh…I don't want** [authority figure's name] **to see this! I'm so embarrassed!**

Have the authority figure walk about halfway up the aisle and ask: "What's the matter?"

Peek out from behind the kids standing in front, and say: **Oh,** [authority figure's name]**, hi! Um…uh…** [name an adult nearby] **needs to talk to you.** While the authority figure is momentarily distracted, keep trying to frantically clean the mess up with the towels. Say in a stage whisper: **I've got to clean this up!**

The authority figure finally sees what has happened and says: "Oh, [your name], you don't have to do that. Here, let me do it. I'll clean it up. You kids can sit back down. I'll take care of it."

Say: **Oh, no! You're the** [pastor or the VBS Director]. **You have lots of important things you need to be doing. This is my mess—I should clean it up!**

The authority figure picks up a towel and says: "I'll get it. No problem." He or she starts mopping up the mess with the towel.

Say: **Thanks! Wow—that was really nice! I didn't expect you to do that.** Hug the authority figure before he or she leaves the stage and returns to the back of the room.

Say: **Wow, wasn't that awesome? Even though** [authority figure's name] **is a busy** [pastor or VBS director]**, she** [he] **took the time to help me clean up my mess. She** [he] **was so loving and showed love by lending a helping hand.**

That reminds me of what Jesus did. Jesus took the role of a servant and washed his disciples' feet to show the love in his heart for them. Let's sing about the love we have in our hearts for others and how we can lend them a helping hand in the same the way that [authority figure's name] **helped me.**

Have the Treasure Hunt Sing & Play Leader lead the kids in singing "Put a Little Love in Your Heart."

After the song, ask:

Field Test Findings

Children often allow us to peek into the heart of God. When we tested this activity, the Treasure Time Finale Leader didn't even have time to ask kids to come forward. A group of kids spontaneously flooded the stage and began cleaning up the mess! They used towels, the Bible costumes—even their own clothes! Clue Crew Leaders later told us they assumed it was staged—that we'd asked kids ahead of time. Teary-eyed, we shook our heads. The kids were simply living out the Bible Point. They really "got it"!

Day 2

● **What are some ways you can show love to others when you go home?** (Play with my little sister; help my mom make dinner; give my baby brother a bath.)

Have a few kids respond and then say: **Now think of one way you can show love and tell the person sitting next to you about it.** Give kids a few moments to do this, and then say: ✪ **The Bible shows us the way to love!** (Eureka!) **Now let's celebrate what we're learning this week as we sing our theme song.**

Have the Treasure Hunt Sing & Play Leader lead the kids in singing "I've Found Me a Treasure."

Say: **Now let's bow our heads and shut our eyes as we close in prayer.** Pray: **Dear God, thank you for showing us your great love by sending us Jesus. Please help us to show love to one another. Amen.**

✪ BIBLE POINT
A CLUE FOR YOU!
You may want to ask kids how they plan to unlock the keys from the hearts. Since the keys are locked onto the heart, kids will need to help each other unlock the hearts to free the keys. This is a super tie-in to the way Jesus served others, freeing them to share his love.

A CLUE FOR YOU!
Remind kids to leave their magnetic bookmarks, student books, and plastic name badges with their crew leaders.

TREASURE CHEST QUEST

Call a volunteer up to the front to read each Treasure Chest Quest Clue. To build excitement, lead kids in saying "hmm" after each clue is read; then lead them in a "drumroll" and a "trumpet fanfare" as the chest is opened. Use the Treasure Tie-In on page 15 to help kids connect the treasure to today's Bible Point. Then call up the Treasure Hunt Director to give any announcements and dismiss kids in an orderly manner to get their treasures from the treasure chest.

Have preschoolers remain seated until their parents or caregivers come and get them. Distribute their treasures from a second treasure chest.

Play the *Treasure Hunt Sing & Play* audiocassette or CD as kids exit.

BIBLE POINT
✺ The Bible shows us the way to pray.

BIBLE BASIS

John 17:1–18:11. Jesus prays for his disciples and all believers, and then he is arrested.

We can only imagine the power and peace Jesus drew from his times in prayer. How he must have relished those all-too-brief moments—talking with the Father, pouring out his heart, praying for those he loved, and praising God. Perhaps that's why Jesus so often prayed privately, slipping away from the crowds to spend a few intimate hours with the heavenly Father. But this time was different. After the Passover meal, Jesus prayed, allowing his disciples to hear the burdens of his heart. And although the pain and suffering of the Cross were only hours away, Jesus prayed for his disciples and those they would lead. With his eyes turned toward heaven, Jesus spoke words of love and concern, words of finality and unity. In an intimate moment with the Father, Jesus spoke of those he loved and cared for…including you and me.

Although prayer is a key element in a child's relationship with God, praying can be difficult for children to understand or practice. Since they can't see God, children may feel confused about talking with God or disconnected when they try. That's why the kids at your VBS will appreciate today's activities. They'll learn that God really *does* hear our prayers, that we can use simple words when we pray, and that Jesus loved us so much that he prayed for us. Children will experience meaningful and creative prayers to help them discover the joy of spending time with God.

A CLUE FOR YOU!

Kids will love seeing the Chadder Chipmunk™ puppet appear in place of the teddy bear! Chadder is cute and cuddly, and kids will enjoy seeing their mischievous friend in a new setting!

Field Test Findings

You can either have an actor for each role, or you can put on the skit with just two people—one person as the President and one person as the visitors. We had one energetic man playing all of the visitors during the field test—it was a laugh riot! And the entire skit required only two actors! Easy!

A CLUE FOR YOU!

We've provided this script on the *Skits & Drama* audiocassette to make this as easy as possible. However, if you have a group of high schoolers who enjoy drama, you may want to have them act this out without the cassette.

Spotlight on Supplies

For today's treasure hunt, you'll need

- ❍ simple costumes for the "Hailing the Chief" skit. Some costume possibilities include a wig and a scarf for the woman, a sport coat for the man, headphones for the young man, a bathrobe for the sleepy woman, and a baseball cap and teddy bear for the child.
- ❍ a table and two chairs,
- ❍ an audiocassette or CD player,
- ❍ *Treasure Hunt Sing & Play* audiocassette or CD,
- ❍ photocopies of the script "Hailing the Chief" (pp. 29-30) or the *Skits & Drama* audiocassette and a cassette player,
- ❍ simple magnifying glasses (one per child), and
- ❍ two treasure chests.

Spotlight on Setup

Cue the *Skits & Drama* audiocassette to the "Hailing the Chief" segment, and set up the table and two chairs. Lay out the costumes and props "backstage" where they'll be readily accessible. Recruit at least two people as actors in the skit and go over their roles with them ahead of time. If possible, ask one or two people to help with costuming backstage.

It's Treasure Time!

While you're waiting for crews to arrive from their Discovery Sites, say: **While we're waiting for everyone to get here, let's sing some songs! Let's start by singing the song "Where Do I Go?" That way, when people hear us singing, they'll know where to go for our finale!** Lead kids in welcoming the Treasure Hunt Sing & Play Leader and play "Where Do I Go?" Join in as everyone sings and does the motions to this uplifting song. If you're still waiting for kids to arrive, have the Treasure Hunt Sing & Play Leader lead kids in "Jesus Loves Me."

When everyone has arrived, say: **Welcome to Day 3 of our Treasure Time Finale! Today we learned that the Bible shows us the way to pray** (Eureka!) **Let's start by singing "I've Found Me a Treasure." Our verse for today tells us about Jesus praying.** Join in as everyone sings.

Then say: **Now let's watch a skit about an important world leader and people who come to talk to him. As you watch, I'd like you to ask yourself how this is like the way we sometimes talk to God.** Play the "Hailing the Chief" skit from the *Skits & Drama* audiocassette.

HAILING THE CHIEF

NARRATOR: The President sat at his desk in his office, waiting. He waited and waited, even though he had many, many important things to do.

Looking up from his schedule, he smiled. Yes, there *was* a lot to do. But first, some people were coming—some very important people.

At least *he* thought they were very important. That was why he kept inviting them to come to his office and talk with him. He longed to hear what was in their hearts and minds, to talk about how they felt, what they needed, how they could help him accomplish his goals...

SECRETARY'S VOICE: Mr. President, they're here, sir.

PRESIDENT: Ah...send the first one in, please.

NARRATOR: The door opened, and a woman ushered herself into the room. She plopped down in a chair and shut her eyes tight.

WOMAN: *(In a nasal, singsong voice)* Dear Mr. President, thank you for the world so sweet, thank you for the food we eat, thank you for the birds that sing, thank you, sir, for everything. Goodbye.

NARRATOR: Before the President could say a word, the woman opened her eyes, got up, and walked out the door. The President sighed. Why did it always seem to go like this? He pushed the intercom button.

PRESIDENT: Next, please.

NARRATOR: The door opened, and in came a man wearing a suit.

MAN: *(Clasping his hands and looking at the ceiling)* O thou chief executive who art in the capitol. O thou in whom so much doth constitutionally dwell, upon whose desk has been placed a most effective blotter; incline thine ear toward thy most humble citizen and grant that thy many entities may be manifoldly endowed upon the fruitful plain...

NARRATOR: The President closed his eyes and rubbed his head.

MAN: *(In a loud voice)* And may thy thou dost harkeneth whatly didst shalt evermore in twain asunder.

PRESIDENT: Excuse me, but what—

MAN: *(Seeming not to hear)* Goodbye.

NARRATOR: The President sighed again.

PRESIDENT: *(Into the intercom)* Next, please.

NARRATOR: In moments, a young man entered. He was wearing headphones and bobbing up and down to the music of his Walkman.

YOUNG MAN: Hey, prez! *(He ignores the offered hand.)* What's happenin'? Nice place you got here. I'm, like, *so* glad we could have this little chat, you know? You're not bad for an old dude, I guess. You don't bother me, I won't bother you, OK? Well, I gotta go. Hang in there, OK? *(He walks out.)*

PRESIDENT: *(Wearily drumming his fingers on the desk)* Next, please.

NARRATOR: There was a pause. At last, a woman entered slowly. She looked like a sleepwalker—eyes nearly shut, jaw slack, her feet dragging. She yawned and slid into a chair.

(continued)

WOMAN: Dear...Mr....President... *(her head droops)* I know I should talk to you when I'm more...awake...but I've got so many things to do...So...sleepy... There was something I was going to say...What...is...? I was going to say... uh... *(She starts to snore.)*

NARRATOR: The President nudged the sleepy woman to her feet. After she left, he gazed sadly out the window. He pressed his intercom button again.

PRESIDENT: How many do we have left?

SECRETARY'S VOICE: I'm sorry, sir. But as usual, most of the people you sent invitations to said they were too busy to talk. They had to watch TV, wax the car, do the dishes...

PRESIDENT: *(Dejectedly)* Oh. Isn't there anyone out there?

SECRETARY'S VOICE: There is *one*, sir. But...he's just a child.

PRESIDENT: *(Shrugging)* Send him in.

NARRATOR: Moments later, a little boy entered shyly. He looked around the room, his eyes wide.

BOY: Are...are you really the President?

PRESIDENT: *(Smiling and offering his hand)* I really am.

NARRATOR: The little boy reached up and shook the President's hand. Then he sat down, folded his hands in his lap, and waited.

The President watched, amazed, as the boy sat politely for nearly a minute.

PRESIDENT: Isn't there...something you want to tell me? Something you have to recite, or ask for, or say?

NARRATOR: The little boy looked down for a moment, thinking.

BOY: Yes, I guess there is.

PRESIDENT: Well, what is it?

BOY: Thanks for inviting me. That's all.

NARRATOR: When the President heard that, he couldn't seem to say anything for a while. All he could do was smile.

But then they talked and talked and talked for the longest, most wonderful time.

Field Test Findings

This skit was so simple, yet so powerful. It grabbed the hearts and attention of adults as well as children. Our staff even performed it at that day's Group staff meeting!

"Hailing the Chief" is adapted from *Joan 'n' the Whale and Other Stories You Never Heard in Sunday School,* copyright © 1987 by John Duckworth. Used by permission. Permission to photocopy this script from Group's Treasure Hunt Bible Adventure: Treasure Time Finale granted for local church use. Copyright © Group Publishing, Inc., P.O. Box 481, Loveland, CO 80539.

After the skit is over, say: **When we pray, God wants us to talk to him the way the little boy talked to the President—simply and thankfully—the way we talk to our good friends. God is listening to us with love, and he wants to answer us. Now let's sing "Let Us Pray" to help us remember that God wants us to talk to him any time.**

Sing "Let Us Pray" together. When the song is finished, say: **Now let's take a moment to pray silently to God. When you're talking to God, remember to talk to him the way you would talk to a friend. While we're praying, I'll name things and people for you to pray for silently.**

Pray: **Dear God, thanks for listening to us when we pray. Please hear the prayers we silently offer to you. We pray for our families.** Pause. **We pray for our friends.** Pause. **We pray for needy children in Spanish-speaking countries who will receive the Gospel of John.** Pause. **We pray for the people sitting on our right** (pause) **and for the people sitting on our left.** Pause. **Thank you for answering our prayers and thank you for sending us your Son, Jesus. Amen.**

Now let's sing another song about prayer. This one will remind us that we can pray for each other. Sing "Hey Now" together.

TREASURE CHEST QUEST

Call a volunteer up to the front to read each Treasure Chest Quest Clue. To build excitement, lead kids in saying "hmm" after each clue is read; then lead them in a "drumroll" and a "trumpet fanfare" as the chest is opened. Use the Treasure Tie-In on page 16 to help kids connect the treasure to today's Bible Point. Then call up the Treasure Hunt Director to give any announcements and dismiss kids in an orderly manner to get their treasures from the treasure chest.

Have preschoolers remain seated until their parents or caregivers come and get them. Distribute their treasures from a second treasure chest.

Play the *Treasure Hunt Sing & Play* audiocassette or CD as kids exit.

Remind kids to take home their treasure boxes and to leave their name badges with their crew leaders.

BIBLE POINT

❂ The Bible shows us the way to Jesus.

BIBLE BASIS

John 19:1–20:18. Jesus is crucified, rises again, and appears to Mary Magdalene.

Jesus' crucifixion was both a devastating and defining event for his followers. Although Peter, a close friend and disciple, denied knowing Jesus, Joseph of Arimathea and Nicodemus, who had been secret followers, came forward in their faith to bury Jesus. Even Mary Magdalene thought she'd lost her greatest treasure. Seeing the empty tomb, Mary probably assumed someone had stolen Jesus' body. Through her tears, she told the angels, "They have taken my Lord away, and I don't know where they have put him." Jesus, her treasure, was gone, and more than anything Mary wanted to find him. Mary didn't need to search for long. Jesus lovingly called her name, revealing himself and the miracle of his resurrection.

The greatest treasure children can find is Jesus. For in knowing Jesus, children will experience forgiveness, love, and eternal life. However, like Mary, the kids at your VBS may have trouble "seeing" Jesus. Mixed messages from the media, school, and non-Christian friends may confuse kids or mislead them. But just as Jesus called Mary by name, Jesus calls each of us by name, too. He knows the hearts and minds of the children at your VBS. Today's activities will help children discover that Jesus is the greatest treasure of all, and that he's right there, waiting for them with open arms.

Day 4

Spotlight on Supplies

For today's treasure hunt, you'll need
○ an audiocassette or CD player;
○ the *Treasure Hunt Sing & Play* audiocassette or CD;
○ brightly colored slips of paper cut into various shapes (one per child);
○ two large paper bags;
○ a simple costume for the character of Jesus, such as a white sheet and a gold cloth strip to tie around the waist;
○ the *Skits & Drama* audiocassette and a cassette player;
○ "gold" coins (three per child); and
○ two treasure chests.

Use up colored scrap paper such as old church bulletins, VBS schedules, and memos. Simply use a paper cutter to cut them into irregular shapes.

Spotlight on Setup

Recruit a few helpers to hand out the brightly colored slips of paper to crew leaders as they walk in.

Prepare the bags according to the illustrations. Be sure to staple only one side together so the character who plays Jesus can pull back the "open" side.

Arrange to have an adult play the character of Jesus. Rehearse the Treasure Time Finale program with him so he understands his role. Be sure to have this volunteer practice holding the inner bag closed, as shown. After Clue Crew Leaders place their papers in the bag, "Jesus" will discreetly open the inner bag to cover the papers. The papers will seemingly disappear.

While you're waiting for crews to arrive from their Discovery Sites, say: **While we're waiting for everyone to get here, let's sing some songs! Does anyone have a request?** Lead kids in welcoming the Treasure Hunt Sing & Play Leader. Join in as everyone sings.

After everyone has arrived, say: **Welcome to Day 4 of the Treasure Time Finale! We're learning that  the Bible shows us the way to Jesus. (Eureka!) We love Jesus so much that we want him to make his home in our hearts. Let's sing that song now and celebrate Jesus who loves us so much.** Have the Treasure Hunt Sing & Play Leader lead kids in singing and doing the motions to "Make Your Home in My Heart."

 BIBLE POINT

Say: **As you walked into Treasure Time Finale today, your crew leaders were given slips of paper. I'd like the crew leaders to hand out the slips of paper to their crew members now. Make sure everyone has one piece.** Give crew leaders a moment to do this; then double-check that each child has one slip of paper.

Say: **Now I'd like you to hold your slips of paper up high.** Ask:

● **What do you notice about these shapes?** (They're weird; they don't make sense; they're strange.)

Let kids give a few answers and then say: **These papers are all different**

Day 4

sizes, shapes, and colors. Just as there are many different slips of paper, there are lots of wrong things that we do. Let's pretend these slips of paper represent the sin in our lives, such as lying, saying mean things, or stealing. Now let's sing "Oh, How I Love Jesus." As you sing and do the motions, hold your slip of paper in the hand that you use the most. Have the Sing & Play Leader lead kids in singing. Have "Jesus" enter near the end of the song, holding the special bag you created.

After the song, say: The papers got in the way while you were singing the song, didn't they? These papers remind me of sin. Sin gets in the way of our relationship with Jesus. Jesus wants to take all that sin. He wants to get sin out of the way so we can have a wonderful relationship with him.

Now I'd like you to pretend that your slip of paper is one specific sin you are sorry for. Hold on to your sin paper, and let's bow our heads and pray together. Dear God, we're sorry we have sinned. We're sorry for the bad things we've done. We want to give our sin to you. We know you love us and forgive us. Amen.

Now we're going to give those sins to Jesus. I'd like each crew leader to collect crew members' papers. When I motion you forward, I'd like you to bring your crew's sin papers and give them to Jesus. After you've put the papers in the bag, I'd like you to stay up here with me for a moment.

Have crew leaders come up, a few at a time, to put their papers in the bag. Be sure that "Jesus" is holding the inner bag closed. Play the "Jesus Takes Away Our Sins" segment of the *Skits & Drama* audiocassette. Say: In 1 John 2:1, it says: "If anybody does sin, we have one who speaks to the Father in our defense—Jesus Christ, the Righteous One. He is the atoning sacrifice for our sins, and not only for ours but also for the sins of the whole world." After everyone's paper is in the bag, have "Jesus" hold out the bag so kids can see all the "sins" in the bag. Then have "Jesus" discreetly unfold the inner bag so it hides the papers. Say: Psalm 103:12 says, "As far as the east is from the west, so far has he removed our transgressions from us." Transgressions are sins—the wrong things that we do. Jesus takes our sins away. He makes them disappear. Have "Jesus" hold out the bag so kids can see the empty bag.

Say: On a treasure map, an X shows where the treasure is. If you tip that X to one side, it looks like a cross. The cross shows how much God loves us. Because Jesus died on the cross, we can find the treasure of God's love. Now "Jesus" and I will share that treasure with each of the crew leaders. We'll use our fingers to mark their hands with the sign of the cross. As we do that, we'll say "The cross marks the spot. Jesus loves you." Then the crew leaders will go back to their crews and do the same thing to each crew member. For example, a crew

---

A Clue For You!

Have your Sing & Play Leader lead kids in singing "Oh, How I Love Jesus" at least once prior to this activity. That way they'll be familiar with the song and the motions.

Field Test Findings

We discovered that our "Jesus" figure needed to move around the room, both to receive the slips of paper and to show that they had disappeared. Not only did this speed up the process, but it allowed more kids to "ooh and aah" over the "disappearing" sins!

Day 4

leader might say, "The cross marks the spot. Jesus loves you, Emily."

Play the "Cross Messages" segment of the *Skits & Drama* audiocassette. While the music plays, have "Jesus" help you "mark" each crew leader's hand with a simple cross sign as you say, "The cross marks the spot. Jesus loves you, [name]." Then dismiss crew leaders to go and share the sign and message with their crew members.

When each child has received a message and a cross, say: **Now let's sing "Oh, How I Love Jesus" again, this time without the papers. We are forgiven—Jesus takes our sins and makes them disappear. Jesus loves us, and we love Jesus too.**

Join kids in singing "Oh, How I Love Jesus."

Then lead children in prayer. Pray: **Dear God, thank you for Jesus, who takes our sins, forgives us, and loves us. Amen.**

Say: **That's such Good News! Let's celebrate by singing "Good News."** Join kids in singing "Good News."

Say: **Now let's *really* celebrate the Good News! Jesus is alive, and because of Jesus, we can live forever too! Let's sing "He's Alive" as we celebrate!** Join kids in singing "He's Alive."

TREASURE CHEST QUEST

Call a volunteer up to the front to read each Treasure Chest Quest Clue. To build excitement, lead kids in saying "hmm" after each clue is read; then lead them in a "drumroll" and a "trumpet fanfare" as the chest is opened. Use the Treasure Tie-In from page 16 to help kids connect the treasure to today's Bible Point.

Then call up the Treasure Hunt Director to make announcements and dismiss kids in an orderly manner to get their treasures from the treasure chest.

Have preschoolers remain seated until their parents or caregivers come and get them. Distribute treasures from a second treasure chest.

Play the *Treasure Hunt Sing & Play* audiocassette or CD as kids exit.

> If you sense that a child might like to know more about what it means to follow Jesus, refer the child to your church's pastor. Or if you feel comfortable talking with the child yourself, give this simple explanation: **God loves us so much that he gave his Son, Jesus, to die on the cross for us. Jesus died and rose again so we could be forgiven for all the wrong things we do. If we ask him to, Jesus will come into our hearts. He'll always be with us and will help us make the right choices. If we believe in Jesus, someday we'll live with him forever in heaven.**
>
> You may want to lead the child in a simple prayer, inviting Jesus to be his or her Lord. Be sure to share the news of the child's spiritual development with his or her parent(s).

Field Test Findings

What a powerful day! I don't think there was a dry eye among the adults in the room! The kids were quiet and respectful as they waited for their crew leaders to give them a "cross" as a reminder of Jesus' love. And many of the crew leaders got choked up as they passed on this important message to each child. All we could say was "Wow!"

Field Test Findings

Talk about delight! Kids were so excited to discover that they would receive *three* gold coins. It turned out to be a simple way to bring huge smiles to kids' faces!

A CLUE FOR YOU!

Remind kids to take home their Good News Treasure Pouches and to leave their name badges with their crew leaders.

BIBLE POINT

✺ The Bible shows us the way to live.

BIBLE BASIS

Acts 27:1-44. Paul stands firm in his faith, even in a shipwreck.

After Paul came to believe in Jesus, he fervently shared the news of Jesus everywhere he went. In Jerusalem, Paul encountered a group of men who opposed his teachings. These men incited a riot, accusing Paul of teaching false doctrine and of defiling the Temple. In the confusion of the angry mob, Paul was arrested and thrown in prison. The following years included trials, death threats, confused centurions, secret transfers to other prisons, and finally a trip to Rome where Paul could plead his case before Caesar. As if Paul hadn't encountered enough trouble, his ship ran into a violent storm and was eventually shipwrecked! Throughout the ordeal, Paul's faith remained strong. He prayed with other prisoners, encouraged his captors to be courageous, and shared his faith in God with everyone on board. Even in the worst circumstances, Paul's life reflected the power of Christ's love.

Most of the children in your VBS won't encounter the kind of persecution that Paul faced. But they'll face tough decisions, peer pressure, false religions, and secular advice that will challenge their faith. That's why it's important for kids to use God's Word as their map for life, a tool to guide them through the storms and "shipwrecks" along the way. Use today's activities to show children the power in the Bible and to help them discover its usefulness in successfully navigating life's everyday trials.

Day 5

Spotlight on Supplies

For today's treasure hunt, you'll need
- an audiocassette or CD player;
- the *Treasure Hunt Sing & Play* audiocassette or CD;
- slides, a slide projector, and a screen (if you decide to do a slide show);
- poster board;
- markers;
- fifteen balloons;
- string;
- a chirping parrot;
- the *Skits & Drama* audiocassette and a cassette player;
- compasses (one per child);
- two treasure chests;
- Operation Kid-to-Kid posters from the Craft Cave Leader; and
- a treasure chest to hold the Spanish translations of the Gospel of John.

A CLUE FOR YOU!
The chirping parrot is available from Group Publishing or your local Christian bookstore.

Spotlight on Setup

Use colorful poster board to create five posters to correspond with Days 1 through 5. On one side of the first poster, write "B." On the other side, write "trust." On one side of the second poster, write "I," and on the other side, write "love." On one side of the third poster, write "B," and on the other side, write "pray." On one side of the fourth poster, write "L," and on the other side, write "Jesus." Finally, on one side of the fifth poster, write "E," and on the other side, write "live." (Be sure to make the letters big enough for all the kids to see.)

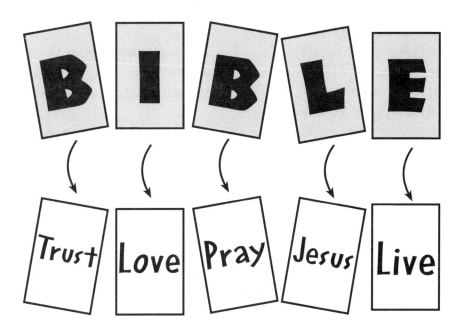

Day 5

A Clue for You!

If you'll be giving the Spanish translations to a church, missionary, or families in your community (instead of to the International Bible Society), it's a good idea to bring photos or video segments of those people to today's Treasure Time Finale. Kids will gain a better understanding of their important offering if they can visualize those who may receive it.

⊛ BIBLE POINT

Field Test Findings

The Treasure Hunt Sing & Play songs are wonderful! Kids loved "request" time, when they could sing their favorites from earlier in the week. Be sure to invite parents to join in the celebration!

Have a volunteer help you blow up the balloons and tie them together in clusters of three.

Ask a few volunteers to come forward to help you demonstrate the chirping parrot.

Arrange for a volunteer to help you usher crews forward for the special offering of the Spanish translations with the Operation Kid-to-Kid bookmarks. Also arrange for two more volunteers to help hand out bunches of balloons and the posters during the end of Treasure Time.

Place a table with a treasure chest on it in the middle of the stage. Right before Treasure Time Finale, get the three Operation Kid-to-Kid posters from the Craft Cave Leader. Attach the posters to sheets of poster board or foam core, then place them around the treasure chest. Kids will bring their Spanish translations forward as an offering, laying them in the treasure chest.

You'll want to test out the chirping parrot ahead of time.

It's Treasure Time

While you're waiting for crews to arrive from their Discovery Sites, say: **While we're waiting for everyone to get here, let's sing some songs! Does anyone have a request?** Lead kids in welcoming the Treasure Hunt Sing & Play Leader. Join in as everyone sings.

After everyone has arrived, say: **Welcome to our final Treasure Time Finale! We've made friends and had a great time this week as we've learned about the Bible, our treasure map. Let's remember all that we've learned this week by singing all five verses of "I've Found Me a Treasure."**

Join kids in singing, and then say: **Today we've learned that ⊛ the Bible shows us the way to live** (Eureka!) **Let's praise God by singing "Got a Reason for Livin' Again."**

Join kids in singing and then say: **One way we show others the love of God in our hearts is by reaching out and helping people. We need to help others know about God's love! We can work together and help each other spread the Good News.**

To see how this works, we're going to try a little experiment.

Hold up the chirping parrot, and say: **I have a little bird here from our rain forest—it's a baby parrot. He's a silent little bird right now. The bird will "peep"—but only when the two metal tabs are touched to make a complete circle.**

Demonstrate how this works by touching each of the metal tabs with one of your fingers. Then remove your fingers from the tabs, and say: **He's not peeping right now. We need to connect with each other and work together.** Ask your volunteers to come up to show how this can work with several people. Touch one finger to one of the metal rings on the bottom of the parrot.

Then join hands with the volunteers to form a circle. The last person in the circle will need to touch the other metal ring.

When you hear the parrot chirp, say: **Let's see what'll happen if we aren't connected with each other.** Have one of the volunteers break the connection and try it again to see if the chirping chick will peep. Then say: **Now let's try to make a connection with the whole group. We'll all be connected together so that we can help each other get the word out. Everyone stand up and join hands. We're all going to work together to get a word out of our bird. Everyone has to be connected to everyone else in this room.** Have crew leaders and other adults help kids all get connected. (If you have parents or other adults who've come early to pick up their kids, this is a great time to get them "connected" as well!)

Say: **Are you ready?** Make the connection to make the chirping parrot chirp.

Say: **Great job! We worked together and helped each other get the bird to peep.** ✪ **The Bible shows us the way to live.** (Eureka!) **God wants us to help each other work together to get God's Word out to everyone. All week long, you've been working together, preparing gospels to give to Spanish-speaking children all over the world. Now we'll bring these books forward as an offering to God.**

In a moment I'll have preschoolers come forward first and place their Spanish translations in this treasure chest. Motion to the treasure chest up front. **Then we'll usher the rest of the crews to bring their books forward, three crews at a time. Each person will bring his or her Gospel of John and place it in the treasure chest. As we do this, we'll all join in singing our favorite Treasure Hunt Bible Adventure songs.**

Begin singing "The B-I-B-L-E," as preschoolers bring their Spanish translations forward. Then take requests from kids for other Treasure Hunt Sing & Play favorites, as you ask all the crews to come forward.

After all of the books are in the treasure chest, say: **Look at all those books! Kids at Treasure Hunt Bible Adventure programs in other towns will prepare gospels, too. When we combine all the books together—it will be a lot! That's thousands and thousands of gospels spreading God's Word.**

Play the "Gracias" segment from the *Skits & Drama* audiocassette. Say: **Let's celebrate all that you've done to spread God's Word to people around the world by singing "He's Got the Whole World in His Hands."**

Join kids in singing and then say: **Give yourselves a hand! Since this is our final Treasure Time Finale, let's review all we've learned this week. I need five volunteers to come up and hold these posters.** Call up five volunteers to hold the posters with the letters facing out. Continue: **Tell me the Bible Point from Day 1.**

As kids shout out the Point, have the first person turn his or her poster

Day 5

A CLUE FOR YOU!

If you have more than 150 children in the room, you may need a microphone near the parrot so everyone can catch the "Wow!" of hearing the chirping sound.

✪ BIBLE POINT

A CLUE FOR YOU!

In case kids aren't all connected (or you're afraid they won't stay connected), use this fail-safe plan to make the parrot "speak." Crowd close to the people up front, and slip your hand behind the person next to you (the person who will touch the other tab). If the bird doesn't chirp, lightly touch that person on the back. You'll make the connection kids will never forget in this activity!

Day 5

Field Test Findings

This Treasure Time Finale took on the feel of a high school pep rally—with kids wildly praising God! It was an awesome way to close out the program and send kids home excited about the treasure they have in Jesus. And they remembered every Point!

around to reveal the word "trust." Continue in this manner until all five Bible Points have been reviewed.

Say: **Now I'm going to need five more volunteers to help me lead "The B-I-B-L-E."** Give each volunteer a balloon cluster, and tell them to hold the balloons high and shake them in time to the music.

Join kids in singing "The B-I-B-L-E."

TREASURE CHEST QUEST

Call a volunteer to the front to read each Treasure Chest Quest Clue. To build excitement, lead kids in saying "hmm" after each clue is read and lead kids in a "drumroll" and a "trumpet fanfare" as the chest is opened. Use the Treasure Tie-In from page 17 to help kids connect the treasure to today's Bible Point.

Then call up the Treasure Hunt Director to make announcements, close in prayer, and dismiss kids to get their treasures from the treasure chest.

Have preschoolers remain seated until their parents or caregivers come and get them. Distribute preschool treasures from a second treasure chest.

Play "I've Found Me a Treasure" as kids exit.